What could George Washington hold
without using his hands?

His breath!

Why is Abraham Lincoln's picture
on the penny?

Because he had so much sense!

What keys won't open any doors
at the White House?

Turkeys, donkeys, and monkeys!

Published by The Millbrook Press, Inc.
2 Old New Milford Road
Brookfield, CT 06804
www.millbrookpress.com

Library of Congress Cataloging-in-Publication Data
Roop, Peter.
Let's celebrate Presidents' Day / by Peter and Connie Roop ;
illustrated by Gwen Connelly.
p. cm.
ISBN 0-7613-1813-5 (lib. bdg.)
1. Presidents' Day—Juvenile literature. [1. Presidents' Day.
2. Presidents 3. Holidays.] I. Roop, Connie
II. Connelly, Gwen, ill. III. Title.
E176.8 .R66 2001
394.261—dc21   00-066428

LET'S CELEBRATE
PRESIDENTS' DAY

By Peter and Connie Roop
Illustrated by Gwen Connelly

The Millbrook Press   Brookfield, Connecticut

FOR HEIDI,
WHO MIGHT SOMEDAY
BECOME PRESIDENT
—PETER AND
CONNIE ROOP

Your teacher puts up pictures of President George Washington and President Abraham Lincoln. There is a special display of books about Lincoln and Washington in the library. No mail is delivered today. Maybe you even have the day off from school. What day is it? Presidents' Day!

Why Do We Celebrate Presidents' Day?

We celebrate Presidents' Day on the third Monday in February to honor George Washington and Abraham Lincoln.

George Washington was our first president. He led the American army to victory in the Revolutionary War. He also helped write the United States Constitution.

Abraham Lincoln was our sixteenth president. He was president during the Civil War. He worked hard to end slavery and to keep the states united.

George Washington was born on February 22, 1732. Abraham Lincoln was born on February 12, 1809. Today we celebrate Presidents' Day between Lincoln's and Washington's birthdays.

Some people wanted George Washington to be king of the United States.

George Washington had false teeth. They were made of ivory, bone, and even hippopotamus teeth.

Lincoln taught himself to read and write.

Abraham Lincoln was our tallest president. He was 6 feet 4 inches tall. He was the first president to grow a beard.

Washington liked cornmeal cakes for breakfast. He also liked crab meat soup, ham, beans, and sweet potatoes with coconut.

George Washington:
Our First President, 1789-1797

George Washington was born on February 22, 1732, on a farm in Virginia. He grew up to be a farmer, soldier, general, and president of the United States. George Washington was over 6 feet tall during a time when most men were an average of 5 feet 4 inches.

He was very serious and courteous. And he was very brave. As a young soldier he took daring risks in battle and was never wounded. Soldiers thought he was an excellent leader.

When the Revolutionary War began, George Washington was chosen to lead the American army against the British. From 1775–1783, he was General Washington. When the war ended, the colonies joined together and became the United States of America. There was only one choice for president, George Washington. He was the only president of the United States who was ever elected unanimously.

Washington was president for two terms (eight years). He then returned to the home

A writer named Parson Weems wrote the first biography of Washington in 1818. He made up a story about George cutting down a cherry tree and telling his father, "I cannot tell a lie, it was I who did it with my hatchet!" Weems wanted people to believe that George was great and noble even as a child. This cherry tree story has become an American legend.

he loved, Mount Vernon, in Virginia. There he lived and farmed until his death on December 14, 1799.

Although he had no children of his own, George Washington is often called the Father of Our Country because he was our first president.

Abraham Lincoln: Sixteenth President, 1861-1865

Abraham Lincoln was born in a log cabin in Kentucky on February 12, 1809. Later, Abe's family lived in Indiana and Illinois.

Abe Lincoln loved to read, play chess, tell jokes, and split wood. He had little time to go to school, but he borrowed many books so he could learn on his own. After he became a lawyer and settled in Springfield, Illinois, Abe was elected to the United States Congress.

People loved hearing Abe tell stories and admired his sense of fair play. In 1860 he was chosen to run for president. The election was bitter. Many people who lived in the South did not like Abe's feelings about ending slavery. During the election, an eleven year old girl wrote to Abe and told him he should grow a beard. He did!

Lincoln won the election and was president during the terrible years of the Civil War. The country was divided over slavery. Most of the southern states wanted to keep slavery. The northern states did not. The Civil War was fought between the northern and southern states. Lincoln believed that the states should be united. Finally, the war ended on April 9, 1865. On April 14, 1865, President Lincoln was shot by John Wilkes Booth. Lincoln died the next day, becoming the first president to be assassinated while in office.

Today Lincoln is remembered as one of our greatest presidents.

Lincoln dreamed about his death the night before he died.

Lincoln once said, "As I would not be a slave, so I would not be a master."

George Washington gave the shortest inaugural speech. He spoke only 166 words!

President William Henry Harrison gave the longest inaugural speech. He spoke on a cold day without wearing a coat or hat. He caught pneumonia and died within a month. His was the shortest presidency.

Half of our presidents were born in only four states: Virginia, Ohio, Massachusetts, and New York.

Six presidents had James as their first name: James Madison, James Monroe, James Polk, James Buchanan, James Garfield, and James "Jimmy" Carter.

Who Can Be Elected President?

Any American can grow up to be president. To serve as president you must be a native-born citizen of the United States, have lived here for the previous 14 years, and be at least 35 years old.

After a president is elected he or she is sworn in at an inauguration ceremony. The ceremony is at noon on January 20. After the inauguration there arc big parties all around Washington, D.C., and a parade down Pennsylvania Avenue.

What Powers Does the President Have?

The president is the commander-in-chief of the armed forces. He has the power to make agreements or treaties with other countries. He often meets with world leaders to discuss problems and find solutions. He can appoint judges and pardon criminals.

Every year the president makes a speech to Congress and the nation called the State of the Union in which he talks about how America is doing.

Can the President Start a War?

ULYSSES S. GRANT
1869–1877

A president cannot declare war. Only Congress can do that. However, no one but the president can order the use of nuclear weapons. Many presidents have fought in wars. Their leadership in battle often led to the presidency.

George Washington was our first general and our first president. He led the United States to victory in the Revolutionary War.

Ulysses S. Grant (1869–1877) became famous as a general who helped win the Civil War. President Grant loved to race horses. One day he got a speeding ticket for racing horses on a Washington street!

Theodore Roosevelt (1901–1909) was a soldier, rancher, author, and explorer. He became well-known for leading his Rough Riders in battle during the Spanish-American War. As president he received the Nobel Peace Prize for helping to end a war between Japan and Russia.

Dwight D. Eisenhower (1953–1961) was the most famous American general of World War II. He was a very popular general and president.

John F. Kennedy was a hero in World War II. When his boat was sunk by a torpedo, he saved the lives of his men even though he had been injured. As president, he dreamed of men walking on the moon. President Kennedy was not alive to see his dream come true because he was assassinated in 1963.

THEODORE
ROOSEVELT
1901–1909

DWIGHT D.
EISENHOWER
1953–1961

JOHN F. KENNEDY
1961–1963

Why Is Washington, D.C., the Capital of the United States?

New York City was the first capital of the United States. Congress met there for only a short time before making Philadelphia the capital in 1790.

After the Revolutionary War, people wanted a new capital. Northern states wanted the capital in the North. Southern states wanted it in the South. So a separate place was decided upon that was not in any state. This area was to be called the District of Columbia (D.C.) in honor of Christopher Columbus.

Congress voted to make the capital along the Potomac River, so President George Washington rode along the river until he found a spot he liked. Maryland and Virginia gave up land for the new district.

The District of Columbia was designed to have wide streets and big buildings. Many parks were made, too, so the city would be inviting. Two men designed the city—Pierre L'Enfant, a Frenchman, and Benjamin Banneker, a free African American. L'Enfant set the Capitol building in a center hub with broad streets coming out from it like spokes on a wheel.

No other building in Washington, D.C., can be higher than the Washington Monument. It is 555 feet tall.

People soon began calling the new city "Washington" to honor George Washington. This embarrassed President Washington, so he called it "Federal City." After Washington died the people had their way, and the name was officially changed to Washington, District of Columbia, or Washington, D.C.

Look at a penny. On one side is President Abraham Lincoln. On the other side is the Lincoln Memorial. Lincoln and his memorial are also on the five-dollar bill.

A picture of the White House is on the $20 bill.

The statue "Freedom" crowns the Capitol dome: Her head is surrounded by lightning rods because she is so often hit by lightning.

Who Was the First President to Live in the White House?

The White House was originally called the President's House. The building was begun in 1792. President John Adams, the second president of the United States, was the first to live there, in 1800. He said, "May none but Honest and Wise Men ever rule under this roof." Abigail Adams, the president's wife, wrote, "This House is built for ages to come." She hung the first painting in the White House, a picture of George Washington.

Mrs. Adams did not like the house very much. Only six rooms were finished. The roof leaked and the walls needed plaster. The rooms were so big that she hung wet laundry in one of them.

In the War of 1812, British soldiers burned the President's House. Dolley Madison, the First Lady, rescued the painting of George Washington before it was lost in the fire. Fortunately, rain put out the fire before the whole building was destroyed.

The President's House was rebuilt and painted white. People began calling it the "White House." In 1902, President Theodore Roosevelt made it official. The president's home would be called the White House.

Every president since Adams has lived in the White House, but not every president liked it.

The White House has a bowling alley, a movie theater, and an indoor pool.

The White House has 132 rooms. Only five rooms of the White House are open to the public.

Thomas Jefferson submitted a design for the White House. His plan was turned down.

President Franklin Roosevelt said, "I never forget that the house I live in belongs to all the people."

The Oval Office, in the White House, is the president's office.

JOHN ADAMS
1797-1801

Do Children Like Living in the White House?

Most presidents' children thoroughly enjoyed themselves in the White House. Some had grand parties. Others had pillow fights while riding tricycles!

President Theodore Roosevelt wrote, "I don't think that any family has ever enjoyed the White House more than we have." And they did! The six Roosevelt children roller-skated down the long halls. They slid down the stairs on serving trays. A favorite game was hide and seek in the White House attic with their father the president (he liked being "It"). They played with their many pets: a bear, a snake, raccoons, dogs, cats, a guinea pig, and a pony. One day they even took the pony in the elevator to cheer up a sick brother!

Willie and Tad Lincoln played games in the big rooms. Tad was nicknamed the Tyrant of the White House because his father let him do almost anything. President Ulysses Grant and his son Jesse spent hours at night on the White House roof looking at stars. John Kennedy Jr. loved to play beneath his father's favorite wooden desk.

President Monroe's daughter Maria was the first president's child to be married in the White House.

President Kennedy created the Children's Garden at the White House.

President Hayes held the first annual Easter Egg Roll on the White House lawn in 1877.

Who Are Some Famous First Ladies?

The president's wife is usually called the First Lady. This tradition began with First Lady Lucy Hayes in 1877.

Dolley Madison was First Lady twice. When her husband James Madison was president (1809–1817) she was the official First Lady. She also helped President Thomas Jefferson (1801–1809) as the White House hostess. Jefferson's wife had died before he was elected president.

Frances Cleveland was the only First Lady to be married in the White House. She married President Grover Cleveland. She was the youngest First Lady we have had (21 years old).

LUCY HAYES

DOLLEY MADISON

When President Woodrow Wilson (1913–1921) was very sick, First Lady Edith Wilson helped him. She kept him informed on what was happening in the world. She told the American people what President Wilson's plans were.

First Lady Jacqueline Kennedy was interested in the arts, and helped Americans see the beauty of their historical treasures.

First Lady Eleanor Roosevelt also helped her husband, President Franklin D. Roosevelt (1933–1945). Mrs. Roosevelt worked hard for equal rights for women. She helped unemployed and poor people. She wrote articles and newspaper stories. First Lady Eleanor Roosevelt was nicknamed First Lady of the World for all of her good works.

FRANCES
CLEVELAND

JACQUELINE
KENNEDY

ELEANOR
ROOSEVELT

What Do Presidents Do After the Presidency?

Former presidents do many different things. George Washington retired to his farm and family. Thomas Jefferson worked to create a college. John Quincy Adams served in Congress for seventeen years.

Andrew Johnson became the only ex-president to serve in the Senate.

President Ulysses Grant and his wife, Julia, traveled around the world. President Grant then wrote a popular book about his life.

President William Howard Taft lost 90 pounds when he retired. He was appointed to the Supreme Court, a job he wanted more than being president!

ULYSSES AND
JULIA GRANT

ANDREW
JOHNSON

President Herbert Hoover helped make the world a better place, especially after World War II. President Jimmy Carter has worked hard for world peace. He uses his skills to help prevent wars. He also works with his wife, Rosalynn, to build homes for poor people.

WILLIAM HOWARD TAFT

JIMMY AND ROSALYNN CARTER

JOHN QUINCY ADAMS

HERBERT HOOVER

George Washington Buttons

During the Revolutionary War many American patriots helped General George Washington by spying on British soldiers. But how did they get the information to the General without getting caught? In Philadelphia, the Darragh family had an idea. At that time, buttons were made of wood. Mrs. Darragh carved out the inside of her son John's coat buttons and placed messages inside. That way John could get past the British guards if they chose to search him.

You can make secret buttons, too.

Here is what you need:

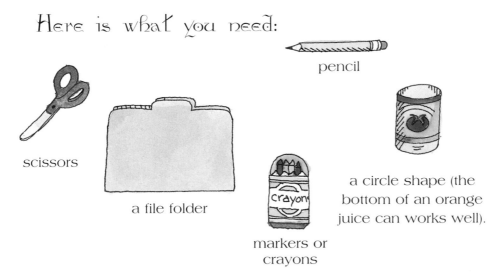

pencil

scissors

a file folder

markers or crayons

a circle shape (the bottom of an orange juice can works well).

stickers or old magazines

1. Place the circle shape on the file folder so it just overlaps the fold. You should be able to trace 3 or 4 buttons from one folder.

2. Trace the circle.

3. Cut out the circle, but make sure you don't cut the fold off.

4. You can decorate your button any way you wish. Make a design with stickers, or draw a picture, or make a collage of pictures from magazines.

5. Using the secret code, write a message inside your button. You might want to write a note to a friend, or send a message to your mom.

This is a simple code. You can make one up that's much harder. To make this work, write out your message and copy it into your button using the matching letters from your code. Have Fun! Szev Ufm!

A = Z
B = Y
C = X
D = W
E = V
F = U
G = T
H = S
I = R
J = Q
K = P
L = O
M = N

N = M
O = L
P = K
Q = J
R = I
S = H
T = G
U = F
V = E
W = D
X = C
Y = B
Z = A

Name the capital of all fifty
states in two seconds.

WASHINGTON, D.C.!

What did Abraham Lincoln lose
every time he stood up?

HIS LAP!

How many sides does the
White House have?

TWO – INSIDE AND OUTSIDE!